To Date or Not To Date …
Guidelines for Christian
Widows and Widowers

To Date or Not To Date—Guidelines for
Christian Widows and Widowers
By Gail Ruth Peterson
Copyright 2011 by Gail Ruth Peterson
Amazon Edition

*We'd like to begin by describing our own dating experience after the loss of our spouses. While we credit God's amazing orchestration in bringing us together, a worthy writing in and of itself to the right audience, our point in telling our story is in the hopes that you will relate to some of our experiences. We also hope our story will encourage everyone to seek God's plan **above** the desire to fill voids and caves of loneliness. Our stories also set the stage for the dating experience by sharing things we learned and took with us into the dating journey—considering aspects of dating that every Christian needs to consider.*

Gail's Story

A few months after Vinnie passed away I was sitting at a traffic light and saw a solider drive by in uniform. I remember asking the Lord, "Would I miss Vinnie with the same deep sadness if he weren't dead but was instead deployed and I was home knowing he'd return home one day? Would it hurt the same? Would I be just as sad?" No sooner did I ask these things did I get my answer. "Gail, you don't have the picture right. He is Home. You are still deployed. Fight the good fight for I [God] still have things for you to do here until it's time for you also to come Home.

In contrast, I often thought of my mother-in-law who was widowed for over 30 years. She remained a widow during those years, vowed to remain dressed in black for the rest of her life. She carried her husband's picture with her where ever she went, visited the grave yard every day to talk to him for hours (except when she visited family in New York. During these times she settled for simply carrying his picture around, talking to it/him and kissing it at night). Reflecting on these two different perspectives of widowhood, I knew that God didn't want me to hold onto Vinnie. He still had a life for me here and I'd see him again in due time.

When the picture of the soldier came to mind, it burned an impression quite different for my life than the one modeled by my mother-in-law. While her faithfulness and loyalty to her late husband was remarkable, I knew the Lord wanted my faithfulness to be in **His** plan for my life now, a plan that did not include Vinnie—I was to be about the Lord's work. I had an image in my mind of Vinnie in Heaven experiencing joy & life like never before. It helped me realize that God wanted me to also experience just as much joy and fullness of life to the best as I am able while I'm here. In other words, it's God's will for both our lives to be lived fully and filled with joy in Him (Vinnie there, me here). I set forth the next year of my widowhood seeking, praying, searching and waiting for God to make this new plan for my life clear to me.

As I began to seek God's purpose for me and eventually felt God nudging me to start some kind of ministry to help widows, I had a number of people ask if I'd also work with widowers. I was asked this enough times that I began to tell God that if He wanted this ministry to include widowers, He'd have to bring a widower in my life because I didn't know any widowers and I didn't know anything about widowers. Though I had absolutely no intention of getting remarried after Vinnie died, that second year as I prayed about God bringing me a widower to partner with me in ministry, I began to entertain the idea of marriage.

The idea that God might have a husband "out there" for me eventually led me to experiment with the Internet. I justified this scary venture by thinking that if I didn't find a new husband this way, I'd at least gain experience about Internet dating that I could pass on and possibly help other widows also pursuing this venue. I learned a great deal about the dangers and scams on Internet dating, gained wisdom about dating at this age (middle aged) AND…I met my second husband!

I thought if God really had a new husband for me and we were to serve in a ministry together, I might as well think and ask BIG! I prayed for a man who was not only retired with enough income that we could both devote our time to ministry but that he'd be more interested in devoting his retirement to ministry work instead of spending the rest of his days traveling and playing golf, and I prayed he would be a widower with a heart for other men struggling in widowhood. Mike was everything I prayed for!

My portion of this booklet comes from what I've learned in this season of my life--from experience, from the Scriptures and some other literary resources. Instead of writing yet another book on the subject, we chose to simplify the subject into this quick-read booklet. We hope that it will lead our readers to their knees, asking the Lord for discernment, wisdom and to be genuinely open to whatever His will is for their individual lives. It's highly recommended that with each step forward, the next step be to stand still for prayer. If so led in prayer to move forward, take the next step and stop for prayer again. There is a good chance that in the process of searching for a potential mate you will get hurt. It's possible that there will be a number of wonderful short-lived relationships that will end for various reasons. It's possible that the Lord will not have you marry again, and in this case, it's our prayer that you will learn this quickly and find peace in whatever other direction the Lord may have for you.

At the same time, I also pray that your falling down a few times by boulders of disappointments won't stop you in your tracks if it's God's will for you to carry on. This is why prayer after each step forward is so important. Only prayer will help you gain the discernment and wisdom you need to know if you are to stop and turn the other way or take another step forward. If there is one tiny nugget of advice I can pass on it would be to **let God be your guide—not your heart!**

Mike's Story

A few months before Linda was diagnosed with brain cancer, I was put on disability due to an injury on my job of 37 years with the phone company. I wondered what on earth I was supposed to do with my life at that point because I knew little else than to work 40-60 hours every week installing phone lines in and around my little community three hours south east of Raleigh. Little did I know that a few months later I'd find myself freed up to take care of my wife on a daily basis as she withered away from cancer in just ten months.

While I was amazed and grateful that I'd been given

the opportunity to care for her every day of her last few months on earth, once she died I began thinking that my life was also over. I was not suicidal but my life no longer had much meaning and purpose. I had no job and no wife. In many ways my life was over.

Looking back I'd have to sum up my first year and a half after Linda's death by describing it as empty. Other than going to church three times a week and occasionally going to lunch after Sunday services (one single man amongst dozens of families and couples) I would sit in my recliner with an end table full of cupcakes, chocolate and brownies eating all day without having to get up. I stared at the TV most of day and into the wee hours of the night watching movies. I even slept most nights in that chair.

After about a year and half of this rather non-existent lifestyle, I began to realize that God wanted more from my life than this. I asked his forgiveness (not for grieving but for my lack of seeking His will for my life). That is when I began to sort of "wake up" from my grief and I asked Him to use me.

It was shortly after this turn in my attitude about life and purpose that I decided that it would be nice to go to dinner once in awhile with someone. I decided to look for a dinner date and subscribed to a couple of Internet dating sites. I never saw myself as getting married again. I wasn't looking for a wife. I really was just tired of dining out with couples and feeling like a third or fifth wheel. I wanted a friend to eat with. Unfortunately, there were few women seeking a simple friendship. Some wanted to get in their bedrooms. Most were looking for a man with money. None of the women I did date gave me much desire to continue meeting them.

Eventually I met Gail and immediately felt like there was something special about her. I loved everything she said about herself and there was just *something* about her picture. I kept looking at her profile trying to figure out what it was that I thought was so special about her. Though marriage was not initially on my radar screen, as I got to know more about her, I quickly began to realize that if I were to get married again, this is the kind of woman I'd want to marry. She was a strong Believer and grounded in God's word, she didn't come with a lot of baggage and problems, and her heart was to serve the Lord all the rest of her days.

We couldn't arrange to meet for three weeks after our initial contact but we spent hours and hours on the phone every day over those three weeks. By the time we met we felt like we knew each other pretty well. Before meeting we were already thinking (and secretly hoping) that God might have put us together and marriage might be in our future.

From our first date in August to our wedding in January, we tried to spend as much time as possible talking about everything we could think of about our past, present, future hopes and dreams, our families, friends, everything we've ever liked to do and described our walk with the Lord over the years. We also, and more importantly, tried to do as many "life-tasks" together as possible—grocery shopping, cooking, housekeeping, worshipping, Bible study and even doctor visits. We felt like we'd learned more about each other in life-tasks than in conversations and eating out. Almost a year into the marriage and we are so thankful we took this route!

Seek First God's Plan

God has a plan for every widowed person. Jeremiah 29:11 "For I know the plans I have for you," declares the LORD, "plans to prosper you and not to harm you, plans to give you hope and a future." This verse is as much a promise to the widowed person as it is to anyone else! This is the most important focus first.

If God's put a desire on your heart to remarry, here are some thoughts to help you think wisely about the pursuit:

God longs for us to know Him as our Heavenly Father (our Maker & Writer of our life story) and our Heavenly Husband. When we find ourselves most broken, most lonely, most in despair that is when God calls us most intensely to know Him in this way. The first year or two of being widowed can be the most significant time in our Christian walk of discovering who God is and who He made us to become in our lifetime! Isaiah 54:5 "For your Maker is your husband— the LORD Almighty is his name— the Holy One of Israel is your Redeemer; he is called the God of all the earth."

If you will allow yourself to find your greatest joy in Him, you will be more open to discerning if "the one" God might have for you is really "the one"! While you/

we wait for a "specific" plan God might have for you/ us, there is always one plan we must continue to fulfill in order to get us there while we wait for the specific plan. 1 Timothy 5:5 tells us, "The widow who is really in need and left all **alone puts her hope in God and continues night and day to pray and to ask God for help**."

Recognize your vulnerability... emotions are intensified in the grief process. This is why being devoted to prayer and a deeper intimacy with the Lord is vital. When our satisfaction is in Him alone, then a new spouse is simply an added blessing but not a necessity to our happiness or completeness. What are healthy and unhealthy motives for seeking a spouse?

- **Loneliness**--while we aren't meant to be isolated this is not a good reason to seek a husband. Deepening the intimacy with Him (God), strengthening friendships or making new encouraging friendships will help ease the vulnerability of loneliness, thus adding wisdom to one's discernment while dating.

- **Replacement**--God knew when you became widowed and He has a plan to help you with all the areas of your life that used to be handled by your spouse. Seek His plan first.

- **Avoiding the time and work to heal from grief**-- prayer and a willingness to work through all the various layers of grief and loss added to a fair amount of time are **all** necessary in the healing process.

- **Work--**For help with the work we recommend GriefShare. There's nothing else out there to help us pick grief apart in bite sizes pieces and help us understand grief and death and the aftermath of its destruction from the lens of Scripture.

- **Time--**Experts advise us that it can take two to five years to fully heal from grief. This time frame may begin months, even years, before the actual death of a spouse with a terminal illness if the surviving spouse planned and prepared ahead. In this case, one year after a spouse dies may be the appropriate time to heal and begin steps for rebuilding their new life.

Am I Free To Marry?

Matthew 22:30 & Mark 12:25 clearly states that there is no marriage after death. "When the dead rise, they will neither marry nor be given in marriage..." If our spouses are not married, neither are we.

1 Corinthians 7:39-40 tells us, "A woman is bound to her husband as long as he lives. **But if her husband dies, she is free to marry anyone she wishes, but he must belong to the Lord.** In my judgment, (Paul's) she is happier if she stays as she is—and I think that I too have the Spirit of God." Paul is recognizing here that it is easier to find joy and one's place in God's work by not taking on the additional role of

spouse and suspects that God would agree but is ALSO not contemning one's desire to remarry.

Paul also recognizes that the desire for intimacy may also be a good reason to pursue marriage when he states in 1 Timothy 5:11, "As for younger widows, do not put them on such a list. (The list is those the church should c are for because they will remain alone without family to care for them or any means of caring for themselves) **For when their sensual desires overcome their dedication to Christ, they want to marry.**"

PLEASE NOTE…Though Paul emphasizes the value of remaining single to do the Lord's work, Mike and I believe we've been able to accomplish more for the Lord's work by being married as opposed to staying single! This matter must be one honestly discerned in prayer.

<u>The Need For Companionship</u>

There is a big difference in today's Western culture, than that of Biblical times, or even that of old European villages like my late mother-in-law. In 30 years of widowhood, she was almost NEVER alone, having plenty of other family members living within walking distance of her home, widows to socialize with and attend church with, and young girls who cared for her, even slept at her home with her, in preparation of their own marriages. Any one of these circumstances is rare for a widow in our culture.

We are not living in the same community that's described in the Bible. Widowed people tend to isolate themselves after losing most of their pre-widow friends who are still married. They have even been found living in a home or apartment for years without a church, friends, family or knowing a single neighbor within miles! Widowed people are most prone to isolation, especially in this society which heightens the need for companionship.

We were made to live in community. If our sense of community was our spouse and our circle of couple friends before losing our spouse, we might feel like a new spouse is the only answer to survival. While some may literally die of loneliness, this is not God's desire, certainly not necessary and it's certainly a wrong reason to remarry before first taking the long journey alone with the Lord unraveling grief.

While almost unbearably painful, grief is a time when the Lord desires to draw us close to Him to fill the voids in our heart and lives. If marriage is pursued before taking the road to healing, one is vulnerable, discernment can be clouded by emotion, wrong expectations can be taken into the marriage which can create tension and baggage that never needs to start at the time of wedding vows.

A good marriage the first time around is not insurance to having a good marriage the second time around. A second marriage can become complicated when the motive on either party is wrong and or grieving from the first spouse has not lead to full healing. Re-establishing one's way into a new sense of community can be a daunting task without the help of those who've paved the way already. Remember, **one doesn't have to pursue marriage to satisfy the search for companionship**. An alternative to marriage could also mean getting a roommate or moving into a community environment (senior apartments are a wonderful option for many!) I had a roommate for six months before marrying Mike. It was a blast, great company and it helped with living expenses too!

Guidelines for choosing a spouse

Be of the same faith. First and foremost be careful to discern that a potential mate is not only of the same foundational faith but also the same spiritual maturity and motivation! If you are a Christian, this passage from 2 Corinthians 6:14-15 should be of the utmost importance for you! "**Do not be bound together with unbelievers**; for what do righteousness and lawless-ness have in common? Or what fellowship has light with darkness or what harmony has Christ with Belial? What has a believer in common with a non believer?"

Pray! Pray! Pray! (and <u>listen</u>!) Pray for the desires of your heart but know what God says in His word.

He's not going to give you the name of the one you may marry again or even tell you that you aren't to re-marry. He tells us to devote ourselves to pray (see 1 Timothy 5:5 above) so He remains our #1 love and source of dependence. We are free to explore the possibilities of God's potential will for us and we'll know if it might be His will if what we do lines up with Scripture. In other words, if we marry a non-Believer hoping we'll one day convert them, we're not in God's will! First the conversion, then the date, then the marriage! If we have sex outside of the marriage, this too is outside God's will.

IMPORTANT NOTE: The topic of sex before marriage is a huge subject. We can't cover this subject in this little booklet alone. However, we will emphasize the fact that widowed people are as single as someone who's never been married. If one is seeking God's will for their life, even if marriage will one day be part of the future, sex before marriage is not. One, it's immoral and the Bible has plenty to say about immorality. Two, it's just plain dangerous! The dangers of sexually transmitted diseases run ramped with people 40+ because of our lack of protection, lack of screening, aged bodies that are more susceptible to disease, and ignorance.

We've added Scriptures at the end of this booklet for you to consider God's view on the subject of sex outside of marriage. Remember, that when asking for and trying to discern God's will, the answer will ALWAYS line up with Scripture so be sure you know what the Scriptures say!

Common interests should be explored. Give yourself time to find areas of interest you may not have been able to explore while married to your spouse and be sure your new potential partner shares common interests. The second marriage can (and many ways should be expected and hoped to be) different than the first. **You should not be looking to repeat life as you knew it before! You will be sorely disappointed!**

Learn who the person really is by the way others relate to them, (not just by what they say). Look deeply into the following relationships:

- **Children/grandchildren:** Ask your potential partner's children about the relationship their parents had. If there was a good marriage before, chances are there won't be concerning issues such as abuse or unfaithfulness to be concerned with.

- **Church family/friends/pastors/elders:** Watch how church members relate to your potential partner. If you are seeking someone who is active in church, you will see the results of this in the relationships built there. Visit Bible study groups that your potential partner is involved in or join your potential partner in some of the areas of ministry he/she might be involved in too, even if only once or twice. This will not only give opportunity to observe involvement and commitment but also to see spiritual gifts and talents put to use.

- **The ability to adopt new family members and incorporate/compromise on each other's family traditions** is vital for keeping us in good relationships with our children and grandchildren. Remember, we may become widowed again and will need the support of our friends and family. Don't isolate from family in order to avoid upsetting a new spouse who's unwilling to incorporate new members or new traditions.

Ability to decide the best place to live and worship. This plan should be decided BEFORE the marriage.

Finances--Learn about debts and spending patterns. Work on a budget together. Discuss thoroughly who will do the finances (although initially do them together!) In the Cushenberys' book referenced at the end, there are suggestions for handling the financial decisions.

Assets/inheritances: It's appropriate to consider how our children might inherit our money, property and assets when we die but these become obstacles when a new spouse enters the picture, especially if he/she too has children and grandchildren to divide the lot with! Mike and I both promised things to our children before we dated which became obstacles when we considered marriage. My promise to give my home to the kids has been changed to an insurance policy instead which has freed me up to live the life God calls me to live, where and with whom He chooses. If I die now the kids won't get the house because it will be where my second husband will live. However, they are beneficiaries of the new insurance policy which is just as simple, if not simpler for them. That was a win/win solution!

Let's Look at Internet Dating: Pros & Cons

Pros: Internet dating can widen one's span of prospects and allow opportunity to get to know someone before meeting, before exposing an address, a real name, or the risk of being alone with a perfect stranger!

Cons:

- May be difficult to find the right person in one's own community
- Run the risk of scams (people looking eventually for monetary benefits)

- May run the risk of "falling" for someone that turns out to be married or married several times

- Long distance relationships heighten the risk of not being able to get to know a potential partner by meeting friends, family, church acquaintances, and financial status. It may also add more difficult challenges to holiday compromises and having to relocate further away from a secure job, friends, a church family, children, grandchildren, and security of community and familiar surroundings. These kinds of changes can put the partner in advantage if they turn out after the marriage to be the controlling type.

- Potential inability to see habitual patterns such as excessive drinking, drugs, partying, unfaithful relationships and/or gambling habits

Only a few years ago, pastors and even some other experts alerted people to the dangers of Internet dating, even suggested it be avoided all together. While there are dangers in Internet dating, there are also great advantages! First, let's look at the pros and cons then we'll look at ways to "play the game" with wisdom and some safety measures in place.

Who else are they interested in? The first man I was interested in was from Mississippi. He was captivated by my writing, a genuine Christian, sincere, respectful, encouraging, had a great job with an obvious good income, loved children, etc. (the list goes on). He was so intrigued with me that it was a real shock when it turned out that he was just as intrigued with someone else. He encouraged me to date other men too which should have been a clue, but I was vulnerable and hopeful and failed to see his point. I was really hurt by his decision to cancel plans to meet me in NC which I learned a week later was because of his greater interest in another.

Beware of "working out of the country" AND "returning in one month". For some reason, these scammers (who are seeking, from best I can tell, vulnerable widows who are so lonely they'll do anything for love, even send money for a "desperate situation"—such a sudden illness in his family or some other emergency). These type scammers like Christian women too! They can talk the talk and walk the walk to fool their prospects! Usually these men (if they really are men) use alias names and write as if they never got past the 2nd grade! Grammar is awful and you'll wonder if they even speak English (& some probably don't!). They won't talk on the phone (saying they can't because of the location of their temporary work assignment). They will also "fall in love with you IMMEDIATELY, hoping you'll believe how much they feel they can't live without you! Bottom line-- **BEWARE of these relationships!!!**

Ask a lot of personal questions! If they are lying, you may catch them not giving the same information twice. Ask for addresses of their US residence if they claim they work outside the country. I looked up an address on WhitePages.com once and saw the resident of that address were quite old and had lived in that house for over 50 years!

Do a back ground check! If you are serious about the dating pursuit, sign up for a membership do conduct background checks online. One with a reasonable cost and of the best reputable is NetDetective.com. BEWARE of background scams too! If they are too cheap you're going to pay something and get nothing! Background checks can help you find out criminal charges, even traffic violations on someone, proof of age and residence too.

Skype or use FaceBook video to communicate. It's easy to write or have someone else write lovely things in an email or even a chat conversation but there's so much more to learn in a face-to-face conversation! Besides, actually talking face to face, even on a computer, can help you "hear" sincerity as well as see what the other person really look like. Pictures on profiles aren't always current and sometimes they are pictures of someone else!

Read between the lines. Reading someone's impressive profile can get exciting but remember, there are people that really "know what to say" to be attractive online. Look for key statements that indicate their "faith" is genuine and lived out daily. Ask them to expand on Christian clichés to see if their statements have substance to them.

The first date can bring up emotions not expected and make you feel like you're not ready. For me, my first date with someone made me face another layer of grief I wasn't expecting until I got face to face with the person! Quitting the pursuit however isn't necessarily the right reaction. Like anything, perseverance will make one wise and open the playing field until Mr. or Mrs. Right comes along—learn as you go!

Suggestions for good sites:

E-Harmony is not the best choice for everyone. It gets good reviews on TV but Mike & I both found it limited. We preferred to be the ones to decide who might be right for us, not a computer.

Match.com is very good because members are able to write a lot of information about themselves on the site and post many pictures. I found it helpful to take time to read thoroughly many profiles initially so I could detect certain repetitive phrases that might indicate copy-cats who couldn't define who they genuinely are. I also wasn't interested in someone who couldn't take the time to write about such an important matter as describing oneself to another potential partner!

ChristianMingle.com is where we found each other. We liked it because there were more Christians on the site looking for other Believers. Here one must exercise caution too though because it is an attractive site for scammers to find what they hope to be "rich and vulnerable widows".

Beware of cheap inexpensive sites! Remember, if a scammer is looking for a monetary gain by being on a dating site he or she is not going to want to pay much for their membership either! These sites are filled with flirt buttons and smile icons. The thought of what the other person was thinking while sending or receiving flirt buttons is hideous! Some might even have a wife tending to a house full of laundry and children while their husband is sending "flirts" to women everywhere they never intend on meeting.

The Bottom Line

Several years ago I was compelled to take on the Children's Ministry program in my home church. I met a lady that had quite a bit of experience working with babies in her church, an age group I wasn't sure how to handle in bulk! I asked her if she would be my part time assistant for a while.

We worked well together for quite a while until one day we worked on a mailing. I asked her to fold the letters a particular way and she went nuts on me. To my surprise, she yelled at me. Yes, right in the office with other people and pastors around. She was upset because I'd hired her to (in her words) tell me how to do things. Mind you, I'd been an administrative assistant for years. Who knew how to fold letters?

I asked her to leave. She never came back. Later my pastor asked me what I learned from the experience. My answer was simple, an answer I have had to fall back on again and again as I've worked with and pray for you that it's the fulfillment of God's plan, a plan we also pray leads to great joy and fulfillment for you and great blessing to others!

<u>**Suggested Resources:**</u>

The Snared by Lois Rabey

Coping With Life After Your Mate Dies
by Donald & Rita Cushenbery

Getting To The Other Side of Grief
by Robert de Vries & Susan J. de Zonnebelt Smeenge

See also the GriefShare.com bookstore for a list of books written specifically for widow people.

Some other Scriptures for consideration:

Sexual immorality

1 Corinthians 6:12-13 "I have the right to do anything," you say—but not everything is beneficial. "I have the right to do anything"—but I will not be mastered by anything. You say, "Food for the stomach and the stomach for food, and God will destroy them both." The body, however, is not meant for sexual immorality but for the Lord, and the Lord for the body.

1 Corinthians 6:18 Flee from sexual immorality. All other sins a person commits are outside the body, but whoever sins sexually, sins against their own body.

1 Corinthians 7:2 But since sexual immorality is occurring, each man should have sexual relations with his own wife, and each woman with her own husband.

Ephesians 5:3 But among you there must not be even a **hint** of sexual immorality, or of any kind of impurity, or of greed, because these are improper for God's holy people.

Colossians 3:5-6 Put to death, therefore, whatever belongs to your earthly nature: sexual immorality, impurity, lust, evil desire and greed, which is idolatry. Because of these, the wrath of God is coming.

1 Thessalonians 4:3-8 It is God's will that you should be sanctified: that you should avoid sexual immorality; that each should learn to control your own body in a way that is holy and honorable, not in passionate lust like the pagans, who do not know God; 6 and that in this matter no one should wrong or take advantage of a brother or sister. The Lord will punish all those who commit such sins, as we told you and warned you before. 7 For God did not call us to be impure, but to live a holy life. 8 Therefore, anyone who rejects this instruction does not reject a human being but God, the very God who gives you his Holy Spirit.

Romans 7:3 So then, if she has sexual relations with another man while her husband is still alive, she is called an adulteress. But if her husband dies, she is released from that law and is not an adulteress if she **marries** another man.

Hebrews 12:16 See that no one is sexually immoral, or is godless like Esau, who for a single meal sold his inheritance rights as the oldest son.

Widows remarrying

1 Timothy 5:11 As for younger widows, do not put them on such a list. For when their sensual desires overcome their dedication to Christ, they want to marry.

1 Timothy 5:14 So I counsel younger widows to marry, to have children, to manage their homes and to give the enemy no opportunity for slander.

Remaining single

1 Corinthians 7:8 Now to the unmarried and the widows I say: It is good for them to stay unmarried, as I do.

1 Timothy 5:5 The widow who is really in need and left all alone puts her hope in God and continues night and day to pray and to ask God for help.

The Widow's Peek

P.O. Box 99672

Raleigh, NC 27624

www.TheWidowsPeek.org
TheWidowsPeek@ymail.com

Made in the USA
Middletown, DE
13 December 2020

27425613R00019